THE GAZE OF THE GORGON

Books available by Tony Harrison

POETRY BOOKS BY TONY HARRISON

Palladas: Poems (Anvil Press Poetry, 1975)
U.S. Martial (Bloodaxe Books, 1981)
Selected Poems (Viking/Penguin, 1984; second edition, 1987)
v. (Bloodaxe Books, 1985; second edition, 1989)
A Cold Coming (Bloodaxe Books, 1991)
The Gaze of the Gorgon (Bloodaxe Books, 1992)

THEATRE POETRY BY TONY HARRISON

Dramatic Verse 1973-1985 (Bloodaxe Books, 1985)
The Mysteries (Faber, 1985)
Theatre Works 1973-1975 (Penguin, 1986)
  – paperback edition of *Dramatic Verse 1973-1985*
The Trackers of Oxyrhynchus (Faber, 1990; second edition, 1991)
  – second edition includes Delphi and Olivier texts of the play
The Common Chorus (Faber, 1992)
Square Rounds (Faber, 1992)

ESSAYS ON TONY HARRISON

Tony Harrison, edited by Neil Astley
  Bloodaxe Critical Anthologies: 1 (Bloodaxe Books, 1991)

THE GAZE OF
THE GORGON

TONY HARRISON

BLOODAXE BOOKS

ISBN: 1 85224 238 8 hardback edition
       1 85224 239 6 paperback edition

First published 1992 by
Bloodaxe Books Ltd,
P.O. Box 1SN,
Newcastle upon Tyne NE99 1SN.

Second impression February 1993.

Bloodaxe Books Ltd acknowledges
the financial assistance of Northern Arts.

Cover printing by J. Thomson Colour Printers Ltd, Glasgow.

Printed in Great Britain by
Cromwell Press Limited, Broughton Gifford, Melksham, Wiltshire.

Acknowledgements

Most of the poems in this book are collected from other publications by Tony Harrison, from pamphlets and from his most recent American collection. Fourteen of the poems were published in *V. and Other Poems* (Farrar Straus Giroux, New York, 1990). *The Guardian* published 'Initial Illumination' on 5 March 1991 and 'A Cold Coming' on 18 March 1991; they were then published by Bloodaxe Books in *A Cold Coming: Gulf War Poems* (1991), with the photograph by Kenneth Jarecke from *The Observer* described in 'A Cold Coming': *'The charred head of an Iraqi soldier leans through the windscreen on his burned-out vehicle, February 28. He died when a convoy of Iraqi vehicles retreating from Kuwait City was attacked by Allied Forces.'*

The sequence of 'Sonnets for August 1945' – part of Tony Harrison's continuing work *The School of Eloquence* – was published in part in *Anno 42* (Scargill Press, 1987), in *V. and Other Poems*, and in *Poetry Review*; 'The Morning After' (I & II) and 'Old Soldiers' appeared in the second edition (1987) of his *Selected Poems* (Penguin Books), and are reprinted as the opening poems in this sequence.

'The Gaze of the Gorgon' is the text of a poem-film first shown on BBC 2 Television on 3 October 1992.

'The Mother of the Muses' was published by Bloodaxe Books in 1991 in *Tony Harrison* (Bloodaxe Critical Anthologies: 1), edited by Neil Astley. 'The Mother of the Muses' and 'Losing Touch' were published in limited, private press editions by Peter Jolliffe and Bob Castle in 1989 and 1990.

Some of these poems also appeared in *The Independent, London Magazine, The London Review of Books* and *Poetry Review*.

Contents

9   Sonnets for August 1945:
       1. *The Morning After*
       2. *Old Soldiers*
       3. *The Figure*
       4. *Black & White*
       5. *Snap*
       6. *First Aid in English*
       7. *The Birds of Japan*

17   The Poetry Lesson
18   Listening to Sirens
19   The Act
22   Y
24   Summoned by Bells
26   Fire & Ice
27   The Icing Hand
28   The Pomegranates of Patmos
36   Broadway
37   Losing Touch
38   The Mother of the Muses
46   Initial Illumination
48   A Cold Coming
57   The Gaze of the Gorgon

Sonnets for August 1945

1. *The Morning After*

I.

The fire left to itself might smoulder weeks.
Phone cables melt. Paint peels from off back gates.
Kitchen windows crack; the whole street reeks
of horsehair blazing. Still it celebrates.

Though people weep, their tears dry from the heat.
Faces flush with flame, beer, sheer relief
and such a sense of celebration in our street
for me it still means joy though banked with grief.

And that, now clouded, sense of public joy
with war-worn adults wild in their loud fling
has never come again since as a boy
I saw Leeds people dance and heard them sing.

There's still that dark, scorched circle on the road.
The morning after kids like me helped spray
hissing upholstery spring wire that still glowed
and cobbles boiling with black gas tar for VJ.

II.

The Rising Sun was blackened on those flames.
The jabbering tongues of fire consumed its rays.
Hiroshima, Nagasaki were mere names
for us small boys who gloried in our blaze.

The blood-red ball, first burnt to blackout shreds,
took hovering batwing on the bonfire's heat
above the *Rule Britannias* and the bobbing heads
of the VJ hokey-cokey in our street.

The kitchen blackout cloth became a cloak
for me to play at fiend Count Dracula in.
I swirled it near the fire. It filled with smoke.
Heinz ketchup dribbled down my vampire's chin.

That circle of scorched cobbles scarred with tar 's
a night-sky globe nerve-rackingly all black,
both hemispheres entire but with no stars,
an Archerless zilch, a Scaleless zodiac.

2. *Old Soldier*

Last years of Empire and the fifth of War
and *Camp* coffee extract on the kitchen table.
The Sikh that served the officer I saw
on the label in the label in the label
continuously cloned beyond my eyes,
beyond the range of any human staring,
down to amoeba, atom, neutron size,
but the turbaned bearer never lost his bearing
and nothing shook the bottle off his tray.
Through all infinity and down to almost zero
he holds out and can't die or fade away
loyal to the breakfasting Scots hero.

But since those two high summer days
the U.S. dropped the World's first A-bombs on,
from that child's forever what returns my gaze
is a last chuprassie with all essence gone.

3. *The Figure*

In each of our Blackpool photos from those years
and, I'll bet, in every family's South Pier snap,
behind the couples with their children on the pier, 's
the same figure standing in frayed suit and cap.

We'd come to plunge regardless in the sea,
ball-shrivellingly chill, but subs all gone,
gorge Mrs Moore's Full Board, now ration-free,
glad when *I-Speak-Your-Weight* showed pounds put on.

The first snap that I have 's from '45.
I've never seen a family group so glad
of its brief freedom, so glad to be alive,
no camera would have caught them looking sad.

He's there, in the same frayed suit, in '51,
that figure in each photo at the back
who sent us all sauntering towards the sun
and the tripod, and the biped draped in black.

4. *Black & White*

If we had the cameras then we've got today
since Oblivion, always deep, grew even deeper
the moment of the flash that made VJ
and the boom made almost pro ones so much cheaper,
I'd have snaps of me happy and pre-teen
in pale, affordable Fuji for the part
of innocence that never could have been
born just in time to see the World War start.

The ugly ducklings changed to sitting ducks!

Now everything gets clicked at the loud clock
the shots and shutters sound like 's Captain Hook's
ticking implacably inside the croc.

If he wants his shadow back the Peter Pan
who cowers since Hiroshima in us all
will have to keep returning to Japan
till the blast-cast shape walks with him off the wall.

5. *Snap*

Uncle Wilf in khaki but decapitated,
and he'd survived the jungle and the Japs,
so his grin 's gone when we all celebrated
Hirohito's empire in collapse.

My shorter father 's all in and looks glad
and full of euphoria he'd never found
before, or since, and I'm with the grocer's lad
two fingers turned the positive way round!

Innocence, that fraying Kirby wire
that briefly held the whole weight of the nation
over the common element of fire
that bonded the A-bomb blast to celebration,
our VJ bonfire to Jehovahspeak,
the hotline Jesus got instructions from,
and, at Pentecost, Apostles their technique
of saying in every language: *Ban the Bomb!*

6. *First Aid in English*

First Aid in English, my first grammar book
with a cross on the light blue cover of dark blue
drilled into a [?] of parrots that one rook
became a congregation when it's two.

We chanted gaggle, bevy, coven, herd
between the Nazi and the Japanese defeat.
Did even the dodo couple have its word
that became, in the last one's lifetime, obsolete?

Collective nouns but mostly bird or beast.
Ghetto and gulag weren't quite current then.
The fauna of our infancies decreased
as new nouns grew collectivising men.

Cats in their clowder, lions in their pride,
but there's no aid in English, first or last,
for a [Fill in the Blank] of genocide
or more than one [Please Tick] atomic blast.

7. *The Birds of Japan*

Campi Phlegraei, Lake Nyos of Wum,
their sulphur could asphyxiate whole flocks
but combustibility had not yet come
to the femto-seconds of the *Fiat Nox*:
men made magma, flesh made fumaroles,
first mottled by the flash to brief mofettes
and Hiroshima's fast pressurising souls
hissed through the fissures in mephitic jets.

Did the birds burst into song as they ignited
above billowing waves of cloud up in the sky,
hosannahs too short-lived to have alighted
on a Bomb-Age Bashō, or a Hokusai?

Apostles of that pinioned Pentecost
of chirrupings cremated on the wing
will have to talk their ghosts down, or we're lost.
Until we know what they sang, who can sing?

The Poetry Lesson

Its proboscis probes the basking monster's eye.
The *Flambeau*, whose ambrosia's salt dew
and nectars sucked from caymans' *lacrimae*,
survives on saurian secretions in Peru.

The blue fritillary of north Brazil
I saw uncurl the watchspring of its tongue
and, by syphoning or licking, have its fill
of goodnesses discarded in man's dung.
The question mark (complete with added dot)
crapped on the pavement in full public view
by cane-hooch-smashed emaciate was steaming hot
but ambrosia not shit to browsing Blue.

Both lessons in survival for fine words
to look for fodder where they've not yet looked –
be lepidoptera that browse on turds
or delicately drain the monster's duct.

Listening to Sirens

Was it the air-raids that I once lived through
listening to sirens, then the bombers' drone
that makes the spring night charter to Corfu
wake me at 2, alarmed, alert, alone?
I watch its red light join the clustered stars
in the one bright clearing in the overcast
then plummet to become a braking car's
cornering deserted side-streets far too fast.

My lilac purples as the headlamps pass
and waft it in, that same lilac smell
that once was used to sweeten mustard gas
and induce men to inhale the fumes of hell.
A thin man from that War who lived round here
used to go berserk on nights like these,
cower, scream, and crap his pants with fear
whenever he scented lilac on the breeze.

Senses that have been blighted in this way
or dulled by dark winter long for the warm South,
some place we hollow out for holiday,
and nothing spoils the white wine in the mouth.
I drag my senses back into the dark
and think of those pale Geordies on their flight.
I'll still be oblivious when they disembark
dazzled by the blue and the bright light.

The Act

(for Michael Longley & James Simmons)

Newcastle Airport and scarcely 7 a.m.
yet they foot the white line out towards the plane
still reeling (or as if) from last night's FED
or macho marathons in someone's bed.
They scorn the breakfast croissants and drink beer,
and who am I to censure or condemn?
I know oblivion 's a balm for man's poor brain
and once roistered in male packs as bad as them.
These brews stoke their bravado, numb their fear
but anaesthetise all joy along with pain.

To show they had a weekend cunt or two
they walk as if they'd shagged the whole world stiff.
The squaddies' favourite and much-bandied words
for describing what they'd done on leave to birds
as if it were pub-brawl or DIY
seem to be, I quote, 'bang', 'bash', or 'screw',
if they did anything (a biggish if!)
more than the banter boomed now at the crew
as our plane levels off in a blue sky
along with half-scared cracks on catching syph.

They've lit Full Strengths on DA 141
despite NO SMOKING signs and cabin crew's
polite requests; they want to disobey
because they bow to orders every day.
The soldiers travel pretty light and free
as if they left Newcastle for the sun,
in winter with bare arms that show tattoos.
The stewardesses clearly hate this run,
the squaddies' continuous crude repartee
and constant button-pushing for more booze.

I've heard the same crude words and smutty cracks
and seen the same lads on excursion trains
going back via ferry from Stranraer
queuing at breakfast at the BR bar,
cleaning it out of *Tartan* and *Brown Ale*.
With numbered kitbags piled on luggage racks
just after breakfast bombed out of their brains,
they balance their empty cans in wobbly stacks.
An old woman, with indulgence for things male,
smiles at them and says: 'They're nobbut wains!'

Kids, mostly cocky Geordies and rough Jocks
with voices coming straight out of their boots,
the voices heard in newsreels about coal
or dockers newly dumped onto the dole
after which the army's the next stop.
One who's breakfasted on *Brown Ale* cocks
a nail-bitten, nicotined right thumb, and shoots
with loud saliva salvos a red fox
parting the clean green blades of some new crop
planted by farm families with old roots.

A card! The stewardesses almost throw it
into our laps not wanting to come near
to groping soldiers. We write each fact
we're required to enter by 'The Act':
profession; place of birth; purpose of visit.
The rowdy squaddy, though he doesn't know it
(and if he did he'd brand the freak as 'queer')
is sitting next to one who enters 'poet'
where he puts 'Forces'. But what is it?
My purpose? His? *What* are we doing here?

Being a photographer seems bad enough.
God knows the catcalls that a poet would get!
Newcastle-bound for leave the soldiers rag
the press photographer about his bag
and call him Gert or Daisy, and all laugh.
They shout at him in accents they'd dub 'pouf'
Yoo hoo, hinny! Like your handbag, pet!
Though what he's snapped has made him just as tough
and his handbag hardware could well photograph
these laughing features when they're cold and set.

I don't like the thought of these lads manning blocks
but saw them as you drove me to my flight,
now khakied up, not kaylied but alert,
their minds on something else than *Scotch* or skirt,
their elbows bending now to cradle guns.
The road's through deep green fields and wheeling flocks
of lapwings soaring, not the sort of sight
the sentry looks for in his narrow box.
'Cursed be dullards whom no cannon stuns'
I quote. They won't read what we three write.

They occupy NO SMOKING seats and smoke,
commandos free a few days from command
which cries for licence and I watch them cram
anything boozable, *Brown Ale* to *Babycham*
into their hardened innards, and they drain
whisky/lemonade, *Bacardi/Coke*,
double after double, one in either hand,
boys' drinks spirit-spiked for the real *bloke*!
Neither passengers nor cabin crew complain
as the squaddies keep on smoking as we land.

And as the morning Belfast plane descends
on Newcastle and one soldier looks,
with tears, on what he greets as 'Geordie grass'
and rakes the airport terrace for 'wor lass'
and another hollers to his noisy mates
he's going to have before their short leave ends
'firkins of fucking FED, fantastic fucks!'
I wish for you, my Ulster poet friends,
pleasures with no rough strife, no iron gates,
and letter boxes wide enough for books.

Y

I'm good with curtains
                    — MRS THATCHER

The thing I drink
from above the earth
's by *Technoplastics Inc.*
(Fort Worth)

I hear the chinks
of pukka glass
from what I think 's
called Business Class,

my taste buds impressed
as bustle helps waft
the Premium repast
to the Y class aft.

Farther fore there's china
and choices for dinner.
The wines get finer,
the glass thinner.

Veuve Cliquot for the man
with a 1st thirst; for me
a tiny ring-pull can
of California Chablis!

From our plastic drinking,
O Ys of all nations,
it's maybe worth thinking
that the one consolation 's:

if the engines fail
and we go into a dive
only Ys in the tail
ever seem to survive!

As the stewardesses serve
first to 1st, last to Y,
I can't fail to observe,
as on earth so in the sky,

that the U.S.A.
draws no drapes –
the First Class can pay
while the Y Class gapes

pour encourager...
any man can fly
Premium if he can pay
(or his company).

We curtain the classes
while they eat,
the plastics from glasses,
we are so discreet!

And from LHR to JFK
from JFK to LHR
things are going to stay
just as they are.

Summoned by Bells

The art of letters will come to an end before AD 2000...
I shall survive as a curiosity.

         − EZRA POUND

O Zeppelins! O Zeppelins!
prayed poet E.P.
any Boche gets 60 pence
to bust this campanolatry!

Doubles, triples, caters, cinques
for corpse or Christmas joys
for him, or anyone who thinks,
may be 'foul nuisance' and mere noise.

Carillons can interfere
and ruin concentration.
I've had it wrecked, my rhythmic ear,
by the new faith of the nation.

So sympathise with E.P.'s plight.
This moment now it's hard to hold
this rhythm in my head and write
while those bloody bells are tolled.

St Mary Abbot's, they're passé.
What gets into my skull
any time of night and day
are the new bells of John Bull,

The new calls to the nation:
Securi-curi-curi-cor!
Join the fight against inflation!
Double-Chubb your door!

'Beat Inflation' adverts call.
Invest in stronger locks!
Display for all on your front wall
the crime-deterrent box.

Almost every day one goes
and the new faith that it rings
is vested in new videos
and the sacredness of things.

24

I got done once. No piercing peal
alerted neighbourhood or force
but then there's nothing here to steal
bar 'a few battered books', of course.

The poor sneak thief, all he could do
he had so little time to act,
was grab a meagre coin or two
and my bag there ready packed.

What bothers me perhaps the most
is I never heard the thief,
being obsessively engrossed
in rhymes of social grief.

In haste behind the garden wall
he unzipped my bag. Bad luck!
One glance told him that his haul
was 50 copies of one book!

Poems! Poems! All by me!
He dropped the lot and ran
(and who would buy hot poetry
from a poor illiterate man?)

deeply pissed by what he'd found,
dumped books and bag unzipped.
He'd've even ditched an Ezra Pound
Cantos manuscript.

I got my books, he went scot-free,
no summons, gaol or fines.
I used him for such poetry
this alarm leaves in these lines

on 'a botched civilisation'
E.P. helped to rebotch
where bells toll for a nation
that's one great Neighbourhood Watch.

Fire & Ice

The dusky, extinct 16 June 1987, Florida

A sprinkler simulates the rain.
A man in Lysolled wellies brings
live larvae to it, crickets, grain,
and the dusky, near extinction, sings.

The dusky in its quarantine 's
the very last there'll ever be.
In a Georgia lab its frozen genes
stay fledged with numb non-entity.

It's mocked up well its habitat.
The meal-supply's well-meaning.
Though there's no mate to warble at
the dusky goes on preening.

So let's be glad that it dropped dead
in that life-affirming mood.
The keeper found its little head
still buried in its food.

The Saxon saw man's spirit fly
like a bird though glowing firelight,
a warmth between two blanks of sky,
a briefly broken night.

Ours could be a dusky clone,
the freezered phoenix of our fate,
that flies, preens, even sings, alone
singed by the sparks from its charred mate.

The Icing Hand

That they lasted only till the next high tide
bothered me, not him whose labour was to make
sugar lattices demolished when the bride,
with help from her groom's hot hand, first cut the cake.

His icing hand, gritty with sandgrains, guides
my pen when I try shaping memories of him
and his eyes scan with mine those rising tides
neither father nor his son could hope to swim.

His eyes stayed dry while I, the kid, would weep
to watch the castle that had taken us all day
to build and deck decay, one wave-surge sweep
our winkle-stuccoed edifice away.

Remembrance like iced cake crumbs in the throat,
remembrance like windblown Blackpool brine
overfills the poem's shallow moat
and first, ebbing, salts, then, flowing, floods this line.

The Pomegranates of Patmos

We may be that generation that sees Armageddon.
— RONALD REAGAN, 1980

My brother, my bright twin, Prochorus,
I think his bright future 's been wrecked.
When we've both got our lives before us
he's gone and joined this weird sect.

He sits in a cave with his guru,
a batty old bugger called John,
and scribbles on scrolls stuff to scare you
while the rabbi goes rabbiting on.

He seems dead to us, does my brother.
He's been so thoroughly brainwashed by John.
'I look in your eyes,' said our mother,
'but the bright boy behind them has gone.'

And the God with gargantuan ΓΡΑΨΟΝ
commanding that crackpot to write
is a Big Daddy bastard who craps on
the Garden of Earthly Delight.

If that sect's idea of a Maker 's
one who'll rid the world of the sea
I'm sitting beside watching breakers
he's the wrong bloody maker for me.

Who believes that their God began it
when he's ready to end it so soon,
the splendours of Patmos, the planet,
and the sea and the stars and the moon?

There'll always be people who'll welcome
the end of the sea and the sky
and wail to their God to make Hell come
and rejoice to hear the damned cry,

a date ringed in red in their diary
when they know that Doomsday will be
sure they'll be safe from the fiery
Gehenna engulfing, among billions, me!

I tell him it's crap, his Apocalypse.
I'm happy here in this world as I am.
I'd sooner wear shorts specked with fig pips
than get all togaed up for the Lamb.

If begged to go up where their Lamb is,
those skyscrapers of chrysolyte,
kitted out in a cloud-issue chlamys,
with no darkness, then give me the night,

night with its passion and peril,
Patmos with pomegranates and figs
not towerblocks built out of beryl
and glazed with best sardonyx.

When Prochorus comes back from a session
up the hill in the cave with the saint,
he plunges me straight into depression
and, more than once, has made mother feel faint.

All he sees is immediately made
an emblem, a symbol, a fable,
the visible world a mere preaching aid,
even the food mother lays on the table.

An Apocalyptic cock on his heap,
Prochorus crowed as I tried to dine:
'Awake, ye drunkards, and weep,
and howl, all ye drinkers of wine!'

In one of his scrolls envisioning Hell
where the divine allowed him to delve,
in Joel, son of Pethuel
(he added, the pedant, I.12!),

he found a quotation that made his day
and he tried to use to mar mine,
how pomegranates would wither away
and shrivelled grapes hang from the vine.

He tried to convince me but didn't succeed,
as I spiked out the vermilion gel
from the pomegranate, that its seed
stood for the sperm of the Future flame-lit from Hell,

an orb of embryos still to be born,
a globe of sperm globules that redden
not with the glow of the Aegean dawn
but the fires of his God's Armageddon.

My orb of nibbleable rubies
packed deliciously side by side
his roes of doom-destined babies
carmine with God's cosmocide.

The pomegranate! If forced to compare,
to claim back what eschatology stole,
what about, once you've licked back the hair,
the glossed moistness of a girl's hole?

He could take a gem-packed pomegranate,
best subjected to kisses and suction,
and somehow make it stand for the planet
destined for fiery destruction.

But in Kadesh in the deserts of Zin,
I asserted, the children of Israel chode
their leader Moses for dumping them in
what they called an *evil* abode.

They called that place evil, and why?
(Ask your divine, he should know!)
Because the deserts of Zin were dry
so that no pomegranates could grow.

They saw no hope of staying alive
without the fruits you'd love to see blighted
(see NUMBERS XX. 5 –
not bad for one branded 'benighted'!)

Prochorus wasn't prepared for debate.
He and his sort preferred
pouring out endless sermons of hate
and from us not a dicky bird.

The more he went on about how our isle
would vanish along with its ocean
the more I spat kernels and flashed him a smile
and ate more in provoking slow motion.

And what made my brother really rave
and hiccup and spit 666,
what finally sent him back to his cave
were my suckings and sensual licks.

Each seed I impaled I'd hold up high
as though appraising a turquoise,
then with a satisfied sensual sigh
suck off the gel with a loud noise.

Apoplectic with Apocalypse,
his eyes popped watching me chew,
he frothed at the mouth as I smacked my lips
at the bliss of each nibbled red bijou.

So that verse (Rev. XXII.2)
about the fruit tree with 12 different crops
was my brother's addition, if John only knew,
as a revenge for me smacking my chops.

But I knew that I'd never be beaten
by his brayings of blast and of blaze,
and since then, when disheartened, I've eaten
pomegranates to give joy to my days.

And their flowers also are so brave and red,
a redness I've seen intensify
when the storm pressed down and overhead
the darkest clouds massed in the sky.

When the storm clouds bear down their most black,
at the moment the gloom looms most low,
the blown bright balausts bugle back
their chromatic jubilo.

The Doomsday Clock's set at 5 to.
The lovers I follow have time for their stroll
and to let their sensual selves come alive to
the Patmos that gladdens the soul,

the Patmos of figs and pomegranates,
the Patmos of the sea and the shore,
Patmos on earth among planets,
Patmos that's Patmos and no metaphor.

I'm so weary of all metaphorers.
From now on my most pressing ambition 's
to debrainwash all like Prochorus
made Moonies by metaphysicians.

But my poor brother could never respond.
I couldn't undermine his defences.
His brain went before him to the Beyond.
He took all leave of his senses.

My brother's heart was turned to stone.
So my revenge on St John's to instil
in lovers like these, who think they're alone,
the joy John and his ilk want to kill,

and try any charm or trick
to help frightened humans affirm
small moments against the rhetoric
of St Cosmocankerworm.

And I follow them lovingly strolling
by the sea I was always beside
with the breakers that I watched still rolling
though it's 2,000 years since I died.

Though the rubbish that's out there floating
shows these days are far distant from mine,
no one should rush into quoting
St John the Doomsday Divine.

Some can't resist the temptation to preach
'The End of the World Is Nigh'
when they see the shit on the beach
or white dishes scanning the sky.

And the johnnies jostling for sea room
like the eelskins of very sick eels
Prochorus would see as new signs of doom
and the angels halfway through the seals.

My charms are mere whispers in lovers' ears
against the loud St End-It-All
and Prochorus would say my present career 's
like the Serpent's before the Fall.

I know nipples brushed by fingertips
that mole up out of their mound
may not arrest their Apocalypse
but it brings the senses to ground.

Lover and lover, a man and his wife,
so grounded assert the sheer
absolute thisness of sublunar life
and not the hereafter, the *here*.

And maybe senses so grounded
will not always be straining to hear
the moment the trumpets are sounded
when the end of the world is near.

And so subliminally into their Sony
I'll put words that I've long thought obscene,
a dose of that dismal old Johnny
but more as a *Weltschmerz* vaccine,

a charm against all Holocausters
and the Patmos Apocalypse freak
and give them the joys that life fosters –
they go back to work in a week!

I follow them walking arm in brown arm.
I sit near to them in the taverna
whispering pagan words as a charm
against the blight of this isle's World-Burner.

By the beach that's a little bit shitty
what I'll sow in these lovers' brains
is a pop poemegranatey ditty
with six verses but seven refrains:

1–2–3–4–
5–6–7
their silvery fire
is staying in Heaven.

Seven seals, love,
and it's said they're at six.
We're lucky to live
with starlight and sex.

1–2–3–4–
5–6–7
their silvery fire
is staying in Heaven.

The stars shine. The moon wanes.
Your left hand undoes
my 501s.
I count the Pleiades.

1–2–3–4–
5–6–7
their silvery fire
is staying in Heaven.

To hell with St John's
life-loathing vision
when I feel in my jeans
your fingers go fishing.

1–2–3–4–
5–6–7
their silvery fire
is staying in Heaven.

Your turn to count.
My turn to lick
your moistening cunt
like a fig, fig.

1–2–3–4–
5–6–7
their silvery fire
is staying in Heaven.

No stars are falling,
all the figs ripen.
I have a gut feeling
the World's End won't happen.

1–2–3–4–
5–6–7
their silvery fire
is staying in Heaven.

The stars won't fall
nor will the fig.
Our hearts are so full
as we fuck, fuck.

1–2–3–4–
5–6–7
their silvery fire
is saying in Heaven.

Broadway

A flop is when the star's first-night bouquets outlast the show itself by several days.

Losing Touch

(in memoriam George Cukor, died 24.1.83)

I watch a siskin swinging back and forth
on the nut-net, enjoying lunchtime sun
unusual this time of year up North
and listening to the news at five past 1.

As people not in constant contact do
we'd lost touch, but I thought of you, old friend
and sent a postcard now and then. I knew
the sentence starting with your name would end:
'the Hollywood director, died today'.

You're leaning forward in your black beret
from the *Times* obituary, and I'd add
the background of Pavlovsk near Leningrad
bathed in summer and good shooting light
where it was taken that July as *I*'m
the one you're leaning forward to address.
I had a black pen poised about to write
and have one now and think back to that time
and feel you lean towards me out of Nothingness.

I rummage for the contacts you sent then:
the one of you that's leaning from *The Times*
and below it one of me with my black pen
listening to you criticise my rhymes,
and, between a millimetre of black band
that now could be ten billion times as much
and none that shows the contact of your hand.
The distance needs adjusting; just a touch!

You were about to tap my knee for emphasis.

It's me who's leaning forward now with this!

The Mother of the Muses

(In memoriam Emmanuel Stratas,
born Crete 1903, died Toronto 1987)

After I've lit the fire and looked outside
and found us snowbound and the roads all blocked,
anxious to prove my memory's not ossified
and the way into that storehouse still unlocked,
as it's easier to remember poetry,
I try to remember, but soon find it hard,
a speech from *Prometheus* a boy from Greece BC
scratched, to help him learn it, on a shard.

I remember the museum, and I could eke
his scratch marks out, and could complete
the...however many lines there were of Greek
and didn't think it then much of a feat.
But now, not that much later, when I find
the verses I once knew beyond recall
I resolve to bring all yesterday to mind,
our visit to your father, each fact, *all*.

Seeing the Home he's in 's made me obsessed
with remembering those verses I once knew
and setting myself this little memory test
I don't think, at the moment, I'll come through.
It's the Memory, Mother of the Muses, bit.
Prometheus, in words I do recall reciting
but can't quote now, and they're so apposite,
claiming he gave Mankind the gift of writing,

along with fire the Gods withheld from men
who'd lived like ants in caves deprived of light
they could well end up living in again
if we let what flesh first roasted on ignite
a Burning of the Books far more extreme
than any screeching Führer could inspire,
the dark side of the proud Promethean dream
our globe enveloped in his gift of fire.

He bequeathed to baker and to bombardier,
to help benighted men develop faster,
two forms of fire, the gentle one in here,
and what the *Luftwaffe* unleashed, *and* the Lancaster.
One beneficial and one baleful form,
the fire I lit a while since in the grate
that's keeping me, as I sit writing, warm
and what gutted Goethestrasse on this date,

beginning yesterday to be precise
and shown on film from forty years ago
in a Home for the Aged almost glazed with ice
and surrounded by obliterating snow.
We had the choice of watching on TV
Dresden destroyed, then watching its rebirth,
or, with the world outside too blizzardful to see,
live, the senile not long for this earth.

Piles of cracked ice tiles where ploughs try to push
the muddied new falls onto shattered slates,
the glittering shrapnel of grey frozen slush,
a blitz debris fresh snow obliterates
along with what was cleared the day before
bringing even the snowploughs to a halt.
And their lives are frozen solid and won't thaw
with no memory to fling its sparks of salt.

The outer world of blur reflects their inner,
these Rest Home denizens who don't quite know
whether they've just had breakfast, lunch, or dinner,
or stare, between three lunches, at the snow.
Long icicles from the low roof meet
the frozen drifts below and block their view
of flurry and blizzard in the snowed-up street
and of a sky that for a month has shown no blue.

Elsie's been her own optometrist,
measuring the daily way her sight declines
into a growing ball of flashing mist.
She trains her failing sight on outside signs:
the church's COME ALIVE IN '85!
the small hand on the *Export A* ad clock,
the flashing neon on the truck-stop dive
pulsing with strobe lights and jukebox rock,

the little red Scottie on the STOOP & SCOOP
but not the cute eye cast towards its rear,
the little rounded pile of heaped red poop
the owners are required to bend and clear.
To imagine herself so stooping is a feat
as hard as that of gymnasts she has seen
lissom in white leotards compete
in trampolining on the TV screen.

There's one with mashed dinner who can't summon
yet again the appetite to smear
the food about the shrunk face of a woman
weeping for death in her 92nd year.
And of the life she lived remembers little
and stares, like someone playing Kim's Game,
at the tray beneath her nose that fills with spittle
whose bubbles fill with faces with no name.

Lilian, whose love made her decide
to check in with her mate who'd had a stroke,
lost all her spryness once her husband died...
He had a beautiful...all made of oak...
*silk inside...brass handles...*tries to find
alternatives...*that long thing where you lie*
for words like coffin that have slipped her mind
and forgetting, not the funeral, makes her cry.

And Anne, who treats her roommates to her 'news'
though every day her news is just the same
how she'd just come back from *such a lovely cruise*
to that famous island...I forget its name...
Born before the Boer War, me, and so
I'm too old to remember I suppose...
then tries again...*the island's called...you know...*
that place, you know...where everybody goes...

First Gene had one and then a second cane
and then, in weeks, a walker of cold chrome,
now in a wheelchair wails for the Ukraine,
sobbing in soiled pants for what was home.
Is that horror at what's on the TV screen
or just the way the stroke makes Jock's jaw hang?
Though nobody quite knows what his words mean
they hear Scots diphthongs in the New World twang.

40

And like the Irish Sea on Blackpool Beach,
where Joan was once the pick of bathing belles,
the Lancashire she once had in her speech
seeps into Canadian as she retells,
whose legs now ooze out water, who can't walk,
how she was 'champion at tap', 'the flower'
(she poises the petals on the now frail stalk)
'of the ballet troupe at Blackpool Tower'.

You won't hear Gene, Eugene, Yevgeny speak
to nurses now, or God, in any other tongue
but his Ukrainian, nor your dad Greek,
all that's left to them of being young.
Life comes full circle when we die.
The circumference is finally complete,
so we shouldn't wonder too much why
his speech went back, a stowaway, to Crete.

Dispersal and displacement, willed or not,
from homeland to the room the three share here,
one Ukrainian, one Cretan, and one Scot
grow less Canadian as death draws near.
Jock sees a boozer in a Glasgow street,
and Eugene glittering icons, candles, prayer,
and for your dad a thorn-thick crag in Crete
with oregano and goat smells in the air.

And home? Where is it now? The olive grove
may well be levelled under folds of tar.
The wooden house made joyful with a stove
has gone the way of Tsar and samovar.
The small house with 8 people to a room
with no privacy for quiet thought or sex
bulldozed in the island's tourist boom
to make way for Big Macs and discothèques.

Beribboned hats and bold embroidered sashes
once helped another émigré forget
that Canada was going to get his ashes
and that Estonia's still Soviet.
But now the last of those old-timers
couldn't tell one folk dance from another
and mistakes in the mists of his Alzheimer's
the nurse who wipes his bottom for his mother.

Some hoard memories as some hoard gold
against that rapidly approaching day
that's all they have to live on, being old,
but find their savings spirited away.
What's the point of having lived at all
in the much-snapped duplex in Etobicoke
if it gets swept away beyond recall,
in spite of all the snapshots, at one stroke?

If we *are* what we remember, what are they
who don't have memories as we have ours,
who, when evening falls, have no recall of day,
or who those people were who'd brought them flowers.
The troubled conscience, though, 's glad to forget.
Oblivion for some 's an inner balm.
They've found some peace of mind, not total yet,
as only death itself brings that much calm.

And those white flashes on the TV screen,
as a child, whose dad plunged into genocide,
remembers Dresden and describes the scene,
are they from the firestorm then, or storm outside?
Crouching in clown's costume (it was *Fasching*)
aged, 40 years ago, as I was, 9
Eva remembers cellar ceiling crashing
and her mother screaming shrilly: *Swine! Swine! Swine!*

The Tiergarten chief with level voice remembered
a hippo disembowelled on its back,
a mother chimp, her charges all dismembered,
and trees bedaubed with zebra flesh and yak.
Flamingos, flocking from burst cages, fly
in a frenzy with their feathers all alight
from fire on the ground to bomb-crammed sky,
their flames fanned that much fiercer by their flight;

the gibbon with no hands he'd had to shoot
as it came towards him with appealing stumps,
the gutless gorilla still clutching fruit
mashed with its bowels into bloody lumps...
I was glad as on and on the keeper went
to the last flayed elephant's fire-frantic screech
that the old folk hadn't followed what was meant
by official footage or survivors' speech.

But then they missed the Semper's restoration,
Dresden's lauded effort to restore
one of the treasures of the now halved nation
exactly as it was before the War.
Billions of marks and years of labour
to reproduce the Semper and they play
what they'd played before the bombs fell, Weber,
Der Freischütz, for their reopening today.

Each bleb of blistered paintwork, every flake
of blast-flayed pigment in that dereliction
they analysed in lab flasks to remake
the colours needed for the redepiction
of Poetic Justice on her cloud surmounting
mortal suffering from opera and play,
repainted tales that seem to bear recounting
more often than the facts that mark today:

the dead Cordelia in the lap of Lear,
Lohengrin who pilots his white swan
at cascading lustres of bright chandelier
above the plush this pantheon shattered on,
with Titania's leashed pards in pastiche Titian,
Faust with Mephisto, Joan, Nathan the Wise,
all were blown, on that Allied bombing mission,
out of their painted clouds into the skies.

Repainted, reupholstered, all in place
just as it had been before that fatal night,
but however devilish the leading bass
his demons are outshadowed on this site.
But that's what Dresden wants and so they play
the same score sung by new uplifting voices
and, as opera synopses often say,
'The curtain falls as everyone rejoices.'

Next more TV, devoted to the trial
of Ernst Zundel, who denies the Jews were gassed,
and academics are supporting his denial,
restoring pride by doctoring the past,
and not just Germans but those people who
can't bear to think such things could ever be,
and by disbelieving horrors to be true
hope to put back hope in history.

A nurse comes in to offer us a cot
considering how bad the blizzard's grown
but you kissed your dad, who, as we left, forgot
he'd been anything all day but on his own.
We needed to escape, weep, laugh, and lie
in each other's arms more privately than there,
weigh in the balance all we're heartened by,
so braved the blizzard back, deep in despair.

Feet of snow went sliding off the bonnet
as we pulled onto the road from where we'd parked.
A snowplough tried to help us to stay on it
but localities nearby, once clearly marked,
those named for northern hometowns close to mine,
the Yorks, the Whitbys, and the Scarboroughs,
all seemed one whited-out recurring sign
that could well be 'Where everybody goes...'

His goggles bug-eyed from the driven snow,
the balaclavaed salter goes ahead
with half the sower's, half the sandman's throw,
and follows the groaning plough with wary tread.
We keep on losing the blue revolving light
and the sliding salter, and try to keep on track
by making sure we always have in sight
the yellow Day-glo X marked on his back.

The blizzard made our neighbourhood unknown.
We could neither see behind us nor before.
We felt in that white-out world we were alone
looking for landmarks, lost, until we saw
the unmistakable McDonald's M
with its '60 billion served' hamburger count.
Living, we were numbered among them,
and dead, among an incomputable amount...

I woke long after noon with you still sleeping
and the windows blocked where all the snow had blown.
Your pillow was still damp from last night's weeping.
In that silent dark I swore I'd make it known,
while the oil of memory feeds the wick of life
and the flame from it's still constant and still bright,
that, come oblivion or not, I loved my wife
in that long thing where we lay with day like night.

Toronto's at a standstill under snow.
Outside there's not much light and not a sound.
Those lines from Aeschylus! How do they go?
It's almost halfway through *Prometheus Bound.*
I think they're coming back. I'm concentrating...
μουσομητορ 'εργανην...Damn! I forget,
but remembering your dad, I'm celebrating
being in love, not too forgetful, yet.

Country people used to say today's
the day the birds sense spring and choose their mates,
and trapped exotics in the Dresden blaze
were flung together in their flame-fledged fates.
The snow in the street outside 's at least 6ft.
I look for life, and find the only sign 's,
like words left for, or *by*, someone from Crete,
a bird's tracks, like blurred Greek, for Valentine's.

TORONTO,
St Valentine's Day.

Initial Illumination

Farne cormorants with catches in their beaks
shower fishscale confetti on the shining sea.
The first bright weather here for many weeks
for my Sunday G-Day train bound for Dundee,
off to St Andrew's to record a reading,
doubtful, in these dark days, what poems can do,
and watching the mists round Lindisfarne receding
my doubt extends to Dark Age Good Book too.
Eadfrith the Saxon scribe/illuminator
incorporated cormorants I'm seeing fly
round the same island thirteen centuries later
into the *In principio*'s initial I.
Billfrith's begemmed and jewelled boards got looted
by raiders gung-ho for booty and berserk,
the sort of soldiery that's still recruited
to do today's dictators' dirty work,
but the initials in St John and in St Mark
graced with local cormorants in ages,
we of a darker still keep calling Dark,
survive in those illuminated pages.
The word of God so beautifully scripted
by Eadfrith and Billfrith the anchorite
Pentagon conners have once again conscripted
to gloss the cross on the precision sight.
Candlepower, steady hand, gold leaf, a brush
were all that Eadfrith had to beautify
the word of God much bandied by George Bush
whose word illuminated midnight sky
and confused the Baghdad cock who was betrayed
by bombs into believing day was dawning
and crowed his heart out at the deadly raid
and didn't live to greet the proper morning.

Now with noonday headlights in Kuwait
and the burial of the blackened in Baghdad
let them remember, all those who celebrate,
that their good news is someone else's bad
or the light will never dawn on poor Mankind.
Is it open-armed at all that victory V,

46

that insular initial intertwined
with slack-necked cormorants from black laquered sea,
with trumpets bulled and bellicose and blowing
for what men claim as victories in their wars,
with the fire-hailing cock and all those crowing
who don't yet smell the dunghill at their claws?

A Cold Coming

'A cold coming we had of it.'
T.S. ELIOT
Journey of the Magi

I saw the charred Iraqi lean
towards me from bomb-blasted screen,

his windscreen wiper like a pen
ready to write down thoughts for men,

his windscreen wiper like a quill
he's reaching for to make his will.

I saw the charred Iraqi lean
like someone made of Plasticine

as though he'd stopped to ask the way
and this is what I heard him say:

'Don't be afraid I've picked on you
for this exclusive interview.

Isn't it your sort of poet's task
to find words for this frightening mask?

If that gadget that you've got records
words from such scorched vocal chords,

press RECORD before some dog
devours me mid-monologue.'

So I held the shaking microphone
closer to the crumbling bone:

'I read the news of three wise men
who left their sperm in nitrogen,

three foes of ours, three wise Marines
with sample flasks and magazines,

three wise soldiers from Seattle
who banked their sperm before the battle.

Did No. 1 say: God be thanked
I've got my precious semen banked.

And No. 2: O praise the Lord
my last best shot is safely stored.

And No. 3: Praise be to God
I left my wife my frozen wad?

So if their fate was to be gassed
at least they thought their name would last,

and though cold corpses in Kuwait
they could by proxy procreate.

Excuse a skull half roast, half bone
for using such a scornful tone.

It may seem out of all proportion
but I wish I'd taken their precaution.

They seemed the masters of their fate
with wisely jarred ejaculate.

Was it a propaganda coup
to make us think they'd cracked death too,

disinformation to defeat us
with no post-mortem millilitres?

Symbolic billions in reserve
made me, for one, lose heart and nerve.

On Saddam's pay we can't afford
to go and get our semen stored.

Sad to say that such high tech's
uncommon here. We're stuck with sex.

If you can conjure up and stretch
your imagination (and not retch)

the image of me beside my wife
closely clasped creating life...

(I let the unfleshed skull unfold
a story I'd been already told,

and idly tried to calculate
the content of ejaculate:

the sperm in one ejaculation
equals the whole Iraqi nation

times, roughly, let's say, 12.5
though that .5's not now alive.

Let's say the sperms were an amount
so many times the body count,

2,500 times at least
(but let's wait till the toll's released!).

Whichever way Death seems outflanked
by one tube of cold bloblings banked.

Poor bloblings, maybe you've been blessed
with, of all fates possible, the best

according to Sophocles i.e.
'the best of fates is not to be'

a philosophy that's maybe bleak
for any but an ancient Greek

but difficult these days to escape
when spoken to by such a shape.

When you see men brought to such states
who wouldn't want that 'best of fates'

or in the world of Cruise and Scud
not go kryonic if he could,

spared the normal human doom
of having made it through the womb?)

He heard my thoughts and stopped the spool:
'I never thought life futile, fool!

Though all Hell began to drop
I never wanted life to stop.

I was filled with such a yearning
to stay in life as I was burning,

such a longing to be beside
my wife in bed before I died,

and, most, to have engendered there
a child untouched by war's despair.

So press RECORD! I want to reach
the warring nations with my speech.

Don't look away! I know it's hard
to keep regarding one so charred,

so disfigured by unfriendly fire
and think it once burned with desire.

Though fire has flayed off half my features
they once were like my fellow creatures',

till some screen-gazing crop-haired boy
from Iowa or Illinois,

equipped by ingenious technophile
put paid to my paternal smile

and made the face you see today
an armature half-patched with clay,

an icon framed, a looking glass
for devotees of "kicking ass",

a mirror that returns the gaze
of victors on their victory days

and in the end stares out the watcher
who ducks behind his headline: GOTCHA!

or behind the flag-bedecked page 1
of the true to bold-type-setting SUN!

I doubt victorious Greeks let Hector
join their feast as spoiling spectre,

and who'd want to sour the children's joy
in Iowa or Illinois

or ageing mothers overjoyed
to find their babies weren't destroyed?

But cabs beflagged with SUN front pages
don't help peace in future ages.

Stars and Stripes in sticky paws
may sow the seeds for future wars.

Each Union Jack the kids now wave
may lead them later to the grave.

But praise the Lord and raise the banner
(excuse a skull's sarcastic manner!)

Desert Rat and Desert Stormer
without scars and (maybe) trauma,

the semen-bankers are all back
to sire their children in their sack.

With seed sown straight from the sower
dump second-hand spermatozoa!

Lie that you saw me and I smiled
to see the soldier hug his child.

Lie and pretend that I excuse
my bombing by B52s,

pretend I pardon and forgive
that they still do and I don't live,

pretend they have the burnt man's blessing
and then, maybe, I'm spared confessing

that only fire burnt out the shame
of things I'd done in Saddam's name,

the deaths, the torture and the plunder
the black clouds all of us are under.

Say that I'm smiling and excuse
the Scuds we launched against the Jews.

Pretend I've got the imagination
to see the world beyond one nation.

That's your job, poet, to pretend
I want my foe to be my friend.

It's easier to find such words
for this dumb mask like baked dogturds.

So lie and say the charred man smiled
to see the soldier hug his child.

This gaping rictus once made glad
a few old hearts back in Baghdad,

hearts growing older by the minute
as each truck comes without me in it.

I've met you though, and had my say
which you've got taped. Now go away.'

I gazed at him and he gazed back
staring right through me to Iraq.

Facing the way the charred man faced
I saw the frozen phial of waste,

a test-tube frozen in the dark,
crib and Kaaba, sacred Ark,

a pilgrimage of Cross and Crescent
the chilled suspension of the Present.

Rainbows seven shades of black
curved from Kuwait back to Iraq,

and instead of gold the frozen crock's
crammed with Mankind on the rocks,

the congealed geni who won't thaw
until the World renounces War,

cold spunk meticulously jarred
never to be charrer or the charred,

a bottled Bethlehem of this come-
curdling Cruise/Scud-cursed millenium.

I went. I pressed REWIND and PLAY
and I heard the charred man say:

THE GAZE OF THE GORGON

a film poem for BBC Television

Exactly 100 years ago in 1892 the marble statue of a dissident German Jewish poet, rejected by his fatherland, was taken by Elizabeth, Empress of Austria, to a retreat in Corfu. The poem film follows its fortunes through the century from its eviction from the island by the German Kaiser, who bought the palace after the Empress was assassinated in 1899, to its present resting place at Toulon in France.

Once established in Corfu, the Kaiser claimed that while Europe was preparing for war he was excavating the 5th century BC pediment which featured a giant Gorgon. The film poem takes this terrifying creature of legend who turns men to stone as a metaphor for what the Kaiser unearthed onto our century, and finds her long shadow still cast across its closing years.

Clutched in the left hand of the marble Heinrich Heine the Kaiser evicted from Corfu is the manuscript of '*Was will die einsame Träne*', a lieder set to music by Schumann. The song in various transformations makes the same journey as its hounded author.

To the same degree, though in different fashion,
those who use force and those who endure it are turned to stone.
SIMONE WEIL: *The Iliad, or the Poem of Force*

Art forces us to gaze into the horror of existence, yet without
being turned to stone by the vision.
FRIEDRICH NIETZCHE: *The Birth of Tragedy*

Ask General Schwarzkopf who Goethe and Schiller
and Heine were. He would be well advised to answer
if he wants to go on addressing Chambers of Commerce
at $50,000 a pop, 'were they the outfield of the
St Louis Cardinals in 1939?'
KURT VONNEGUT

Gulf – Tank Gorgon / Golden Sea	From long ago the Gorgon's Gaze stares through time into our days. Under seas, as slow as oil the Gorgon's snaky tresses coil. The Gorgon under the golden tide brings ghettos, gulags, genocide.
ECU-Land – (Frankfurt)	That's maybe the reason why so many mirrors reach so high into the modern Frankfurt sky.
	ECU-land seems to prepare to neutralise the Gorgon's stare. But what polished shields can neutralise those ancient petrifying eyes?
Goethe statue, Frankfurt	Great German soul, most famed Frankfurter on his plinth, the poet Goethe. Born Frankfurt but deceased Weimar where his mortal remnants are. The old Cold War used to divide where he was born from where he died but now they're once more unified.
Wide shot Schiller statue	And once more it doesn't seem so far from Frankfurt-am-Main back to Weimar. And but an amble down an avenue to Friedrich Schiller on full view and I suppose I ought to say it's right they're put on proud display (though often scorned although their scale 's, say, 50 times this can of ale). It's proper that the Fatherland should give them monuments so grand but there's another German who is quite the equal of those two (and greater in some people's eyes!) whose monument's a fifth their size.

There are, I think, 3 reasons why
my statue's not so bloody high:
1. I was subversive; 2.
(what's worse to some) I was a Jew
and 3. I'm back here almost hidden
because I was 10 years bed-ridden
with syphilis; this keep-fit freak
scarcely suits my wrecked physique.
This monument that's far more humble
's to the voice you're hearing grumble
that he's less on public view,
Heinrich Heine, poet and Jew.

Two grander monuments were planned
but turned down by the Fatherland,
though to the horror of the Habsburg court,
both had the Empress' support
Elizabeth of Austria, Sissy who
felt inspired by the soulful Jew
(but to be frank I wouldn't quote
the poems she claimed my spirit wrote!).
In 1892
Sissy took me to Corfu,
and statues Germany rejected
found safer spots to be erected
and with a more appealing view
of sea and cypress in Corfu
and, like many another hounded Jew,
the second statue found its way
to safe haven in the USA.

Your average Frankfurt-am-Mainer
doesn't give a shit for Heine,
(nor come to that the young mainliner!).
So elbowed to one side back here
surrounded by junked junkies' gear
I, Heinrich Heine, have to gaze
on junkies winding tourniquets
made from the belt out of their jeans,
some scarcely older than their teens.
The Gorgon has them closely scanned
these new lost souls of ECU-land.
The Gorgon's glance gives them their high
then, trapped in her gaze, they petrify.

Schumann Lieder
(Soprano)

Ach, meine Liebe selber
Zerfloß wie eitel Hauch!
Du alte, einsame Träne,
Zerfließe jetzunder auch!

Schumann set those words I wrote
that might bring lumps into your throat
(unless you grabbed for the remote!).
And even if you turned away
you could still hear the *lieder* play.
The marble Heine Deutschland banned
had this *lieder* in his hand,
a manuscript whose crumpled folds
a war-cracked index finger holds.
Where the statue goes the song goes too.
I took it with me to Corfu.
And wish to God I was still there
not here with bloodstains in my hair.
Europe's reluctant to shampoo
the gore-caked coiffure of the Jew,
the blood gushed from a botched injection,
in case it gives it some infection,
or maybe Europe doesn't care
there's junkies' blood in Heine's hair.

The gaze of modern Frankfurt's glued
to this glassy-eyed high altitude.
The Europe of the soaring cranes
has not seen fit to cleanse these stains
or give new hope to the stainer.

(Soprano)

Was will die einsame Träne?

What is the music that redeems
desperate kids in such extremes?
Do those I hope you're watching need a
Schumann setting of my *lieder*?
'This lonely tear what doth it mean?'
we might well ask in such a scene.
Gaze and create. If art can't cope
it's just another form of dope,
and leaves the Gorgon in control
of all the freedoms of the soul.

62

I can do nothing, even cry.
Tears are for the living eye.
So weep, you still alive to shed
the tears I can't shed, being dead.
And if I could I'd shed my tears
that in the century's closing years
the nations' greatest souls preside
over such spirit-suicide,
and that in 1992
Schiller, Goethe, Heine view
the new banks rising by the hour
above a park where chestnuts flower
whose canopies you'd think might cover
lunch-time lounger, reader, lover
but for one who wrestles on his own
against the Gorgon who turns men to stone
the tree with white May blossom sways
like snakes that fringe the Gorgon's gaze,
the serpents that surround her stare.

Spring blossom hisses like her hair,
as this young junkie tries to choose
which vein today is best to use.

Frankfurt police
    The junkies' early evening high
is cut short by the *Polizei*,
who read the law they half-enforce,
and let some shoot-ups take their course.

The regular police routine
is shift the junkies in between
Schiller and Goethe every day
and pass by Heine on the way.

From Schiller's statue back to Goethe's
watching smartly dressed Frankfurters
enter the theatre, and dogs divide
the opiate from the Opera side.

The horns tune up the dogs bark '*raus*'
the precincts of the opera house,
the maestro's rapturous ovations
kept safe by *Polizei* alsatians.
They glimpse a shoot-up then they go
for their own fix of *Figaro*,

see heroin addicts then go in
to hear heroes sing in *Lohengrin*,
and evening junkies grouped round Goethe
hear distorted *Zauberflöte*.
Music is so civilising
for the place with new banks rising.
The main financial centre
of the EEC has to present a
fine *Turandot, Bohème, Cosí,*
for the European VIP.
Traviata, Faust, Aida,
even Schumann's setting of my *lieder*,
just to show, although it's mine,
I can put my own work on the line
and ask as the opera's about to start
what are we doing with our art?

Are we still strumming the right lyre
to play us through the century's fire?

'Bankfurt' they call it; by the way,
I was a banker in my day
and had a somewhat brief career
as Harry Heine banker here
but the banks have grown and rather dwarf
the Jewish poet from Düsseldorf
Not only me. Banks in the skies
cut even Goethe down to size.

With clouds of coins, cash cumuli
floating in the foyer sky
gliding guilder, hard ECU
dream clouds of 1992
you'd think that this Opera House foyer's
a long way from the Gorgon's gaze.
Escape, they're thinking, but alas
that's the Gorgon in the glass.

The ECU bank-erecting crane
reflected in van windowpane,
where, afraid of Aids, the youngsters queue
to trade old needles in for new,
though higher and higher into the blue
new banks to house the hard ECU

rise into the Frankfurt skies,
piece by piece, like Gorgon's eyes
or polished shield of one who slays
the Gorgon, but can't kill her gaze.

Schumann Lieder
(Soprano)

Was will die einsame Träne?
Sie trübt mir ja den Blick.
Sie blieb aus alten Zeiten
In meinem Auge zurück.

Sie hatte viel leuchtende Schwestern,
Die alle zerfloßen sind.
Mit meinen Qualen und Freuden,
Zerfloßen in Nacht und Wind.

Wie Nebel sind auch zerflossen
Die blauen Sternelein,
Die mir jene Freuden und Qualen
Gelächelt ins Herz hinein.

Ach, meine Liebe selber
Zerfloß wie eitel Hauch!
Du alte, einsame Träne,
Zerfließe jetzunder auch!

Corfu shrine of
HEINRICH HEINE:

Isn't this a somewhat finer
monument to Heinrich Heine?
Banished from the Fatherland
with pen and *lieder* in my hand.
The *lieder* Schumann makes so touching
is in this manuscript I'm clutching,
and though war breaks round the manuscript
my hand will always keep it gripped.
But I'll have 10 years of peace
with my Empress here in Greece
from this year 1892,
when Sissy brought me to Corfu.
It was fun to have the Empress fawn
on one so much more lowly born
and so notorious a despiser
of King and Emperor and Kaiser
those Krauts in crowns who used to squat
on Europe's thrones but now do not

wherever history's been rewritten
that's everywhere but backward Britain,
but then I always found the English mind
compared to Europe's lagged behind.

My shrine was in the forest glade
and up above she had displayed
Apollo with the lyre that plays
the darkness out of our dark days
in old times when Apollo's lyre
could save men from the petrifier.

For Sissy these weren't mere antiques
these Muses of the ancient Greeks.
All the human spirit uses
to keep life's colour were the Muses
or at least to Philhellenes like her
and many of her age they were.

She retired from the Imperial Court
into art and poetry, music, thought
though I really wouldn't care to quote
the poems she claimed my spirit wrote
most of her lines are deadly dull
but in all her soul is 'like a gull'
or 'swallow' like the ones that flew
around her Muses in Corfu
and though a palisade of peace
surrounded Sissy and myself in Greece
it was nonetheless a palisade
where Sissy thought and wrote and played.

Music Room
Schumann Lieder
(piano)

How would all these Muses fare
when dragged screaming by the hair
to gaze into the Gorgon's stare?

Dying Achilles
by Ernst Herter
(1884)

The fatal wound, the calf, the thigh
of Achilles who's about to die.
This hero of Homeric fame
gave Elizabeth's retreat its name.
This Achilles of 1884
foresees the future world of war
and shows the Empress half aware
of horrors brewing in the air.

Triumph of Achilles
by Franz Matsch

Schumann Lieder
(piano only)

Her presentiment and pity shows
in the Achilles that she chose,
helpless, unheroic, dying
watching clouds and seabirds flying
and not one so-called 'Eternal Being'
the Gorgon gulls us into seeing.
First the dead man's gaze goes rotten
then flies feast, then he's forgotten
after those who used to shed
their tears for him are also dead
unless a bard like Homer brings
the dead redemption when he sings.
Along with me the Empress/versifier
revered blind Homer and his lyre
the ancient poet whose ILIAD
was the steadiest gaze we'd ever had
at war and suffering Sissy thought
before the wars this century's fought.
Though melancholic, steeped in grief
the Gorgon was a mere motif
for Sissy who was unafraid
to have the Gorgon's face portrayed
on ironwork or balustrade,
and this almost charming Gorgon stares
from wardrobe doors and boudoir chairs,
but unwittingly they laid the track
that brought the grimmer Gorgon back

The palace style based on Pompei's
might warn us of the Gorgon's gaze
but as her century drew to its close
still found poems in the rose,
the lily of loss and grieving hearts
until this closing century starts.
The Empress posed above those roses
vanishes as her century closes
and the Muses she believed in threw
their roses to...I don't know who.
All the century's fresh bouquets
decayed beneath the Gorgon's gaze
the grimmer Gorgon simply waited
till Sissy was assassinated

in the century's closing year,
which brought the German Kaiser here.
And when the Kaiser's gaze met mine
contemplating in my shrine,
the Kaiser's eye began to harden:
I don't want his kind in my garden.
He said straightaway: *Get rid*
of Sissy's syphilitic Yid!
Dammit! the man's a democrat
I've got no time for shits like that.
So once more the poet refugee
was crated up and put to sea.
The crating up I had to face
the Kaiser wished on all my race.

And as the Kaiser wasn't keen
on Sissy's sentimental scene
of Achilles dying he'd make him stand
and represent the Fatherland.
He didn't like this sculpture much.
He liked his heroes much more butch,
more in his own imperious style.
He'd build an Achilles men could HEIL!

'Build my Achilles armour clad'
the Kaiser said, 'and confident in steel
not some mama's little lad
with an arrow in his heel.

Make the wounded warrior stand
regrip his spear and gaze
through Sarajevo to the Fatherland,
the Lord of all that he surveys.

And put a Gorgon on his shield
to terrify his foes
wherever on Europe's battlefield
the Kaiser's Gorgon goes
and that is almost everywhere
as gazers freeze in stony sleep
seeing her eyes and coiling hair
hissing like chlorine gas at Ypres.'

Triumphant Achilles
(statue)
by Johannes Götz
(1909)

68

The Kaiser though a Homer freak
despised the victim and the weak
and looking at Sissy's picture saw
Achilles riding high in war
for him the focus of the painting
was triumph not some woman fainting
but Sissy always used to see
Hector's wife, Andromache,
who has to gaze as Achilles hauls
her dead husband round Troy's walls.
The soon to be defeated rows
of Trojans watch exultant foes
who bring the city to the ground
then leave it just a sandblown mound,
but the Greeks who'll watch Troy blaze
are also in the Gorgon's gaze,
the victims and the victimiser,
conquered and the conquering Kaiser,
Greeks and Trojans, Germans, Jews,
those who endure and those who use
the violence, that in different ways
keeps both beneath the Gorgon's gaze.
A whole culture vanished in the fire
until redeemed by Homer's lyre.
A lyre like Homer's could redeem
Hector's skull's still echoing scream

Statue of
ACHILLES:

Not like Sissy's Achilles sculpted dying
this one's triumphant, time defying.
The crane has hauled into the skies
the Kaiser in Homeric disguise
(though not that you would recognise!)
Not only does this monster dwarf
the dissident from Düsseldorf
now newly banished from Corfu
it dwarfs all Sissy's Muses too.
What can lyre play or bard recite
the same scale as such armoured might
to face his gaze and still create?
Boxed up again inside a crate,
and forcibly reshipped
but still with pen and manuscript,

the shore receding, my last view
of my brief haven in Corfu,
hearing as cypresses recede a
fading phrase of my faint *lieder*,
was Achilles' spear whose gilded tip's
the Kaiser's signpost to Apocalypse.
Which of us, the marble Jew
the Kaiser kicked out of Corfu,
or armoured giant, him or me
would make it through the century?

The founder of the 'master race'
put this inscription on its base.
Those cavities in secret braille
say: *all the Kaiser's work will fail!*
but, wrought in characters of weighty lead,
these pockmarks in the plinth once read:
'The greatest German to the greatest Greek.'
Though not quite equal in physique
the Kaiser's there in his creation,
emblem of his war-like nation,
this bellicose, Berlin-gazing totem
has hornets nesting in his scrotum.
Envenomed hordes have gone and built
their teeming nests in Prussia's kilt,
and perforate the scrotal sac
of the tutued 'Teutomaniac'.

Kaiser excavation
stills

But while all this trouble 's brewing
what's the Prussian monarch doing?
We read in his own writing,
how, while all Europe geared for fighting,
England, Belgium, France and Russia
but not of course his peaceful Prussia,
what was Kaiser Wilhelm II
up to? Excavating in Corfu,
the scholar Kaiser on the scent
of long lost temple pediment
not filling trenches, excavating
the trenches where the Gorgon's waiting
there in the trench to supervise
the unearthing of the Gorgon's eyes.

This isn't how warmongers are
this professor in a Panama
stooping as the spades laid bare
the first glimpse of her snaky hair.

The excavator with his find
a new art treasure for mankind.

The patient Kaiser, piece by piece,
prepares the Gorgon for release
the Gorgon he let out to glower
above us all with baleful power.

Barbitos

The *barbitos*, the ancient lyre,
since the Kaiser's day,
is restrung with barbed wire
Bard's hands bleed when they play
the score that fits an era's scream,
the blood, the suffering, the loss.
The twentieth century theme
is played on barbed wire *barbitos*.

Terpsichore –
Achilleon

Terpsichore the muse who sees
her dances done by amputees.
How can they hope to keep her beat
when war's destroyed their dancing feet?
Shelled at the Somme or gassed at Ypres
they shuffle, hobble, limp and creep
and no matter what old air she plays
they can't escape the Gorgon's gaze.

Melpomene
with tragic mask

The tragic mask of ancient days
looked with eyes that never close
straight into the Gorgon's gaze
and sang Man's history through its throes.

But now where is she when we need her.
Tragedy's masks have changed their style.
Lips like these won't sing my *lieder*.
They've forgotten how to smile.

What poems will this mouth recite?
There'll be no Schumann sung from this.
Before these Germans went to fight
they'd been beautiful to kiss.

71

This is the Kaiser's Gorgon choir
their petrifaction setting in,
grunting to the barbed wire lyre
gagging on snags of *Lohengrin*.

With glaring eyes and hound-like snarls
from the maze-bound Meanderthals
the Kaiser's Gorgon will preside
over ghettos, gulags, genocide.
Mankind meanders through the maze
made rigid by the Gorgon's gaze.
Following a more flowing shape
might find us freedom and escape
from the Gorgon and her excavator
who gears his kind for horrors later.
The Kaiser couldn't stand one Jew
in marble near him in Corfu
but the Kaiser's not uncommon views
were just as vicious on all Jews:
'A poison fungus on the German oak'
(to quote the bastard makes me choke!)
This is how the Gorgon blinds
her henchmen's eyes and rigid minds.

Arrow motif
on pediment

The Gorgon worshippers unroll
the barbed wire gulags round the soul.
The Gorgon's henchmen try to force
History on a straighter course
with Gorgonisms that impose
fixities on all that flows,
with Führer fix and crucifix
and Freedom-freezing politics.
Each leader on his monstrous plinth
waves us back into the labyrinth
out of the meander and the maze
straight back into the Gorgon's gaze.
The Kaiser in his notebook drew
where the Gorgon leads us to
step by step and stage by stage
he steers the Gorgon through our age.
Her hand on his unlocks the door
that never will quite close on War.

The junkie and the nationalist
both get their fixes with clenched fist.
And even in the ECU-world
the Kaiser's flag's once more unfurled.

Ocean borne bodies
and Nazi flag

My statue, meanwhile, got away
with swastikas daubed on my face
out of Hamburg to Marseilles
to Toulon and a new safe base.

And apart from finger, nose and pen
my statue's pretty much intact
but those that let the Gorgon out on men
are totally broken and cracked.

Statues of Gorgon's
henchmen being
demolished –
montage

HEINE's statue
in Toulon:

My statue, meanwhile, got away
with swastikas daubed on my face
out of Hamburg to Marseilles
to Toulon and a new safe base.

And apart from finger, nose and pen
my statue's pretty much intact
but those that let the Gorgon out on men
are totally broken and cracked.

Banished from the Fatherland
still with my *lieder* in my hand
though the pen the poems flowed from
was shattered by an air-raid bomb,
so being without it I recite
as I do now what I can't write.
The *lieder* Schumann makes so touching
is in the manuscript I'm clutching.
This manuscript with faded writing
survived a century of fighting.
Though war broke round this manuscript
my broken hand has kept it gripped.

Toulon lieder
Schumann arr.
Kiszko

No longer hunted or hounded
and safe and fear from fear.
If all the dogs are silenced
why do my eyes shed this tear?

The tears I let fall on the journey
were falling for all I saw.
Today I gaze on the ocean
so far from the fear of war.

The gloom that surrounds those frozen
beneath the Gorgon's gaze
now falls as the century's shadow
to darken our hearts and days.

And though I gaze in sunlight
on springtime's brightest hues,
no longer hunted and hounded
I weep for six million Jews.

(End lieder)

But when through dappled shades of green
I catch glimpses of a submarine,
and across the ocean have to face
through waving palms a naval base,
it's then I'm reassured to know
that just a hundred years ago
when this rejected marble Jew
escaped with Sissy to Corfu
my other monument made its way
to safe haven in the USA,
safe from Europe's old alarms
into the New World Order's arms.

The Bronx,
New York

The Gorgon who's been running riot
through the century now seems quiet,
but supposing one who's watched her ways
were to warn you that the Gorgon's gaze
remains unburied in your day.
I've glimpsed her even in the USA.
You'll all reply he's crying wolf,

Gulf War

but in the deserts of the Gulf
steel pediments have Gorgon's eyes
now grown as big as tank wheel size
that gaze down from her temple frieze
on all her rigid devotees.

74

Skull – lieder Schumann arr. Kiszko (soprano)	The closing century's shadow has darkened all our years and still the Gorgon's filling my empty sockets with tears.
	The tears I let fall in the desert the sand has all soaked away. My eyes and all that they gazed on are gone from the light of day.
	They've gone with these palls of blackness the smoking desert blaze. Will all of our freedoms and glories end up in the Gorgon's gaze?
(end lieder)	O so much life has vanished in smoking fiery skies. The closing century's shadow is cast across all our eyes.
Triumph of Achilles (detail)	The empty helmet of one whose eyes have gone to feast the desert flies, the eyes of one whose fate was sealed by Operation Desert Shield. They gazed their last these dark dark sockets on high-tech Coalition rockets
Tourists	Soon, in 1994, in this palace Greece starts to restore, in this the Kaiser's old retreat Europe's heads of state will meet, as the continent disintegrates once more into the separate states that waved their little flags and warred when the Kaiser's Gorgon was abroad. So to commemorate that rendezvous of ECU statesmen in Corfu I propose that in that year they bring the dissident back here,
End credits	and to keep new Europe open-eyed they let the marble poet preside......
Painter in the Achilleon singing	

V.

SECOND EDITION: WITH PRESS ARTICLES

TONY HARRISON

The Star: 'A plan to televise a poem packed with obscenities caused outrage last night. ITV chiefs intend to screen a reading of Tony Harrison's verse "V" which is full of four-letter words.'

Daily Mail: 'A torrent of four-letter filth...the most explicitly sexual language yet beamed into the nation's living rooms...the crudest, most offensive word is used 17 times.'

GERALD HOWARTH, MP: 'It's full of expletives and I can't see that it serves any artistic purpose whatsoever.'

MARY WHITEHOUSE: 'This work of singular nastiness.'

HAROLD PINTER: 'The criticism against the poem has been offensive, juvenile and, of course, philistine.'

BERNARD LEVIN: 'One of the most powerful, profound and haunting long poems of modern times...A meticulously controlled yell of rage and hope combined, a poisoned dart aimed with deadly precision at the waste of human potential, shaped by a master poet with a rich and instinctive feel for the language, a penetrating eye that misses nothing it looks on, and an exceptionally ingenious capacity for using word-play to make a telling case.'

In the *Newcastle Journal*, David Isaacs linked the attacks on Channel Four's film of v. to 'politically motivated hysteria' and to recent government cutbacks in arts funding, political appointments at the BBC and threats of institutionalised censorship.

The political and media reaction to v. would make a book in itself. Here it is. As well as Tony Harrison's poem and Graham Sykes's photographs, this new edition of v. includes press articles, letters, reviews, a defence of the poem and film by director Richard Eyre, and a transcript of the phone calls logged by Channel Four on the night of the broadcast.

Channel Four's film of v. won the Royal Television Society's best original programme award.

Paperback: ISBN 0 906427 97 5   £5.95   80 pages

Tony Harrison

BLOODAXE CRITICAL ANTHOLOGIES: 1

EDITED BY NEIL ASTLEY

Tony Harrison is both a major social poet and an innovative dramatist. This is the first critical guide to his work, and covers his poetry, translations, theatre, opera and television work:

• Essays and articles by leading writers and critics: Jonathan Barker, Rosemary Burton, Maureen Duffy, Douglas Dunn, Peter Forbes, Mary Garofalakis, Damian Grant, Romana Huk, Peter Levi, John Lucas, Marianne McDonald, Blake Morrison, Oswyn Murray, Bernard O'Donoghue, Carol Rutter, Rick Rylance, Oliver Taplin, Jeffrey Wainwright, Ken Worpole and Alan Young.

• Working with Tony Harrison: articles by director Richard Eyre, designer Jocelyn Herbert, actors Barrie Rutter and Jack Shepherd, composer Stephen Edwards, and TV producers Andree Molyneux and Peter Symes.

• Important reviews of his poetry and plays by John Barber, Clive Barnes, Michael Billington, Michael Coveney, Robert Cushman, Terry Eagleton, James Fenton, Marilyn Hacker, Ian Hamilton, Bernard Levin, John Peter, Michael Ratcliffe, Lawrence Sail, John Simon, Stephen Spender and others.

• Eight essays and prefaces by Tony Harrison as well as his new long poem *The Mother of the Muses*, and the complete texts of his television poems *Arctic Paradise* and *The Blasphemers' Banquet*.

• Interviews with Tony Harrison by John Haffenden and Richard Hoggart.

'A 500-page bumper book...exciting, unstuffy, entertaining and copiously informative' – ROBERT CRAWFORD, *Independent on Sunday*

'Bloodaxe deserves credit for an intelligent introduction to the work of this distinguished, distinctive poet' – PATRICIA CRAIG, *TLS*

Hardback:	ISBN 1 85224 079 2	£25.00	512 pages
Paperback:	ISBN 1 85224 080 6	£10.95	

Dramatic Verse
1973-1985
TONY HARRISON

Tony Harrison's bold and brilliant versions of classics (Molière, Racine, Aeschylus) both respect and so transform them that they have come to be regarded as original pioneering pieces of modern theatre. His National Theatre *Oresteia* has been called 'the best acting translation of Aeschylus ever written' (*TLS*).

His *Misanthrope* has been played by theatre companies throughout the English-speaking world since its National Theatre première in 1973, and has itself been re-translated into other languages, and even back into French.

Dramatic Verse includes verse drama, opera librettos and music theatre, and contains the full texts of *The Misanthrope* (1973), *Phaedra Britannica* (1975), *Bow Down* (1977), *The Bartered Bride* (1978), *The Oresteia* (1981), *Yan Tan Tethera* (1983), *The Big H* (1984) and *Medea: a sex-war opera* (1985).

Hardback: ISBN 0 906427 81 9   £20.00   448 pages

U.S. Martial
TONY HARRISON

Eighteen Martial satires in contemporary (un)dress, their targets the latter-day Romans on New York City. These versions by Tony Harrison, one of modern English poetry's most accomplished and versatile translators, render Martial's Latin vernacular into the fruity argot of the Big Apple.

'*U.S. Martial* shows the opposite side of Harrison's literary make-up. Dismissive, scatological satire suits him as readily as political wit and point-scoring, elegy or meditation' – DOUGLAS DUNN

Pamphlet: ISBN 0 906427 29 0   £2.95   24 pages

Tony Harrison was born in Leeds in 1937. He spent four years in West Africa and a year in Prague before returning to Britain to become the first Northern Arts Literary Fellow in 1967-68, a post he again held in 1976-77. His first collection of poems, *The Loiners*, was awarded the Geoffrey Faber Memorial Prize in 1972. His version of Aeschylus's *Oresteia* won him the European Poetry Translation Prize in 1982, and he was President of the Classical Association in 1987-88. He lives in Newcastle upon Tyne. A full account of his life and work by Rosemary Burton is available in Neil Astley's critical anthology, *Tony Harrison* (Bloodaxe, 1991).

His collections of poems and translations include: *The Loiners* (London Magazine Editions, 1970); *Palladas: Poems* (Anvil, 1975); *From 'The School of Eloquence' and other poems* (Rex Collings, 1978); *Continuous* (Rex Collings, 1981); *A Kumquat for John Keats* and *U.S. Martial* (both Bloodaxe Books, 1981); *Selected Poems* (Penguin/ Viking, 1984; second edition, 1987); *The Fire-Gap* (Bloodaxe, 1985); *v.* (Bloodaxe, 1985; new enlarged edition, 1989); *v. and Other Poems* (Farrar, Straus & Giroux, New York, 1990); *A Cold Coming* (Bloodaxe, 1991); and *The Gaze of the Gorgon* (Bloodaxe, 1992).

Tony Harrison is Britain's leading theatre and film poet. He writes for the National Theatre, the New York Metropolitan Opera, BBC Television and Channel Four. His *Dramatic Verse 1973-1985* (Bloodaxe Books, 1985) includes verse drama, opera librettos and music theatre, and contains the full texts of *The Misanthrope* (1973), *Phaedra Britannica* (1975), *Bow Down* (1977), *The Bartered Bride* (1978), *The Oresteia* (1981), *Yan Tan Tethera* (1983), *The Big H* (1984) and *Medea: a sex-war opera* (1985). *The Mysteries* (Faber, 1985), his adaptation of the English Mystery Plays, was premièred at the National Theatre in 1985. His play *The Trackers of Oxyrhynchus*, which incorporates the remains of Sophocles' satyr play *The Ichneutae*, was first performed in the ancient stadium of Delphi in 1988, and opened at the National Theatre in 1990; the Delphi text was published by Faber in 1990, and both versions appear in the 1991 second edition. His anti-nuclear reworking of the *Lysistrata* of Aristophanes, *The Common Chorus*, was published by Faber in 1992. His latest play, *Square Rounds* (Faber, 1992), opened at the National Theatre in 1992.

His television and film work includes: *Arctic Paradise* (1981) and *The Blasphemers' Banquet* (1989), published in the Bloodaxe critical anthology *Tony Harrison*; his music drama, *The Big H* (1984); Channel Four's film of his poem, *v.* (1987); the BBC series *Loving Memory* (1987); his latest film poem, *The Gaze of the Gorgon* (1992); and screen adaptations of *The Oresteia, The Mysteries* and *Yan Tan Tethera*.